Living in Urban Communities

by Kristin Sterling

first step nonfiction

Lerner Publications Company · Minneapolis

Welcome to my **community**.

A community is a place
where people feel at home.

I live in an **urban** community.

Urban communities are
called cities.

There are many things to
see in a city.

Let's take a look around!

I see many tall buildings.

I see people from around
the world.

I see buses and cars in
the streets.

I see sidewalks and
streetlights.

I see people going to work
in the buildings.

I see people eating at restaurants and shopping.

I see my **neighbor.**

She lives in the **apartment** next door.

Cities are busy and fun.

Do you live in a city?

Ways to help in your community:

Pick up litter.

Plant flowers or vegetables in a community garden.

Be respectful and friendly to your neighbors.

Sweep the sidewalks.

Donate things you don't use to people who can use them.

Urban Facts

 Tall buildings in cities are called skyscrapers.

 Cities are often surrounded by smaller communities called suburbs.

 Urban communities cover only a small amount of the land in the United States.

 There are more people living in New York City than in any other city in the United States.

Urban planners are people who design cities.

 Tokyo, Japan, is one of the biggest cities in the world.

 Very small cities are called towns.

 These towns have funny names:
- Bigfoot, Texas
- Bumble Bee, Arizona
- Dinosaur, Colorado
- Happy Camp, California
- Sandwich, Massachusetts

Glossary

 apartment – one or more rooms in a building used as a place to live

 community – a place where people live together and feel at home

 neighbor – a person who lives near your home

 urban – a community that has little open land and many people

Index

The photographs in this book are used with the permission of: © Dave Nagel/Taxi/Getty Images, cover, p. 17; © Nossa Productions/Riser/Getty Images, pp. 2, 3, 22 (second from top); © PhotoDisc Royalty Free by Getty Images, pp. 4, 22 (bottom); © Lee Snider/Photo Images/ CORBIS, p. 5; © age fotostock/SuperStock, pp. 6, 10; © Randy Faris/CORBIS, p. 7; © Mitchell Funk/Photographer's Choice/Getty Images, p. 8; © Mario Tama/Getty Images, p. 9; © AA World Travel Library/Alamy, p. 11; © Rolf Bruderer/CORBIS, p. 12; © Jean-Pierre Lescourret/CORBIS, p. 13; © Simon Watson/Taxi/Getty Images, pp. 14, 22 (second from bottom); © Ross M Horowitz/Iconica/Getty Images, pp. 15, 22 (top); © Siegfried Layda/Riser/Getty Images, p. 16; © Sonya Farrell/Riser/Getty Images, p. 19.

Lerner Publications Company
A division of Lerner Publishing Group, Inc.
241 First Avenue North
Minneapolis, MN 55401 U.S.A.

Website address: www.lernerbooks.com

Library of Congress Cataloging-in-Publication Data

Sterling, Kristin.
    Living in urban communities / by Kristin Sterling.
        p.   cm. — (First step nonfiction : communities)
    Includes index.
    ISBN 978–0–8225–8597–8 (lib. bdg. : alk. paper)
    ISBN 978–0–7613–3986–1 (eBook)
    1. Cities and towns—Juvenile literature. 2. City and town life—Juvenile literature.
3. City dwellers—Juvenile literature. 4. Communities—Juvenile literature. I. Title.
HT152.S74 2008
307.76—dc22   2007006358

Manufactured in the United States of America
7 – PC – 8/1/13